YOUR NEIGHBOR THE
RACCOON

GREG ROZA

WINDMILL
BOOKS ™

New York

Published in 2012 by Windmill Books, An Imprint of Rosen Publishing
29 East 21st Street, New York, NY 10010

First Edition

Editor: Jennifer Way
Layout Design: Greg Tucker

Photo Credits: Cover, pp. 5, 6, 7 (top, bottom), 8, 9, 10, 11, 12, 13 (top, bottom), 16, 19, 20, 22 Shutterstock.com; p. 4 iStockphoto/Thinkstock; pp. 14–15 Tier Und Naturfotografie J. & C. Sohns/Getty Images; p. 17 Michael Durham/Getty Images; p. 18 Mike Popelyak/Getty Images; p. 21 Hemera/Thinkstock.

Library of Congress Cataloging-in-Publication Data

Roza, Greg.
 Your neighbor the raccoon / by Greg Roza. — 1st ed.
    p. cm. — (City critters)
 Includes index.
 ISBN 978-1-4488-5000-6 (library binding) — ISBN 978-1-4488-5129-4 (pbk.) —
 ISBN 978-1-4488-5130-0 (6-pack)
 1. Raccoon—Juvenile literature. I. Title.
 QL737.C26R69 2012
 599.76'32—dc22
                          2010053726

Manufactured in the United States of America

For more great fiction and nonfiction, go to www.windmillbooks.com

CPSIA Compliance Information: Batch #BS2011WM: For Further Information contact Rosen Publishing, New York, New York at 1-800-237-9932

CONTENTS

WILDLIFE IN THE CITY

When talking about wild animals, many people picture lions, bears, and elephants living in the wilderness. However, there are plenty of wild animals living near people in towns and cities. You might even have raccoons for neighbors!

Raccoons live in the wild, but they have adapted to living in cities and suburbs.

Raccoons are smart animals. They have **adapted** well to life in towns and cities. Raccoons can be hard to find because they are generally active at night, and they sleep during the day. However, signs of raccoons in your neighborhood are easy to spot when you know what to look for.

Raccoons are active mostly at night. You may also see them around dusk or dawn, which would be the beginning and end of the raccoon's "day."

GETTING TO KNOW RACCOONS

Raccoons are **mammals**. Adults can grow to be between 25 and 35 inches (64–89 cm) long. Adult raccoons often weigh between 15 and 25 pounds (7 –11 kg). Most people recognize raccoons because of the masks around their eyes and their ringed tails. Raccoons also have long fingers, which help them catch and eat

This bold raccoon is taking food put out for a family's cats.

Left: The raccoon's eyes let it see things close to it in low light. Its sense of smell is more important for finding its way in the dark, though. *Bottom*: The raccoon's paws work like hands to let the animal catch and handle its food.

prey. In the wild, raccoons can live for up to five years.

As towns and cities grew and the wilderness became smaller, many kinds of animals were forced to move elsewhere. Not raccoons! They adapted to living around people very well.

Raccoons are **omnivores**. That means they eat both plants and animals. They eat just about any food they can get their paws on! Raccoons are known for dunking their food in water before eating it. Scientists are not sure why they do this.

Garbage cans are like supermarkets to raccoons in the city!

In the wild, they eat fish, frogs, bugs, mice, eggs, fruit, and many other things. There is plenty of food for raccoons living in towns and cities. One of their favorite places to eat is in your garbage cans! They will make a mess of your gardens and **compost piles**, too.

The raccoon's paws become more sensitive when wet. This may be one reason raccoons dunk their food in water.

MALE AND FEMALE RACCOONS

Male raccoons usually live alone. However, they will live in a den with a female during the **mating** season. Male raccoons are generally larger than females.

Raccoons are ready to mate when they are about one year old. Mating season is in the winter, between January and

Adult males may form small groups with one another. Related adult females and their young may share feeding or resting places.

March. Males often mate with several females during this time. Females, however, do not mate every year. About 65 days after mating, female raccoons give birth to **litters** of two to five young. This usually happens in April or May. Male raccoons do not help take care of the young.

Female raccoons raise their young without the male.

KITS!

Baby raccoons are called kits. Kits look just like adult raccoons, but they have darker fur. Newborn kits cannot see or walk for about six weeks. They do not come out of their dens until they are between 9 and 12 weeks old.

Mother raccoons are very **protective** of their kits. They carry their

Kits learn how to climb trees during the first year of their lives.

Left: Here is a mother raccoon (center) looking for food with her kits. *Bottom:* There are generally two to five kits per litter.

kits using their mouths when moving to new dens. They teach them how to find food and how to climb trees. Kits stay with their mothers for about a year before moving out on their own.

Raccoons live between southern Canada and northern South America. Most raccoons live in forests where there is plenty to eat. They also tend to live near water, where they can catch fish. Raccoons generally use dens left by other animals in hollow logs and in the ground. Mother

raccoons sometimes build dens high up in trees, where they can keep their families safe.

Raccoons stay active for most of the year. They do not **hibernate** in winter, as animals such as bears do. However, they will sleep in their dens for several days when it is very cold or when their food supply is low.

Mother raccoons may build their dens up in a tree. This helps keep their kits safe.

RACCOONS IN YOUR NEIGHBORHOOD

When raccoons become a problem for homeowners, animal control workers put out traps to catch the animals. They release these raccoons into the wild.

Raccoons like to eat **grubs**, or young insects. They will dig holes in gardens and lawns to find them.

Never leave food out for raccoons! This will only make them want to live nearby.

Raccoons have even made dens in sewer drains!

Raccoons can climb through small holes in houses to make dens under porches and in basements and chimneys.

Make sure your garbage cans are tightly sealed at night. If they are not, raccoons are sure to make a big mess of them!

DANGERS IN THE CITY

Although raccoons do not have to worry about finding food in the city, there are other dangers. In fact, since food and places for dens are often easy to find in a city, raccoons do not have to struggle as they might in the wild. Because of this, overpopulation is

This raccoon found itself trapped in a garbage bin after it climbed in to look for food.

common. Overpopulation, in turn, can lead to a lack of food.

Raccoons often get themselves into trouble searching for food in the city. Some may climb into garbage cans or chimneys and not be able to get back out. Cars also kill many raccoons.

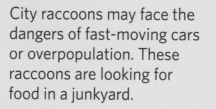

City raccoons may face the dangers of fast-moving cars or overpopulation. These raccoons are looking for food in a junkyard.

RACCOONS AND PEOPLE

City and town raccoons make dens wherever they find space. This might be in a tree, under a porch, or in a woodpile.

As cute as raccoons look, it is important to be careful around them. Do not ever get close to one. Mother

Raccoons sometimes make a den in attics. This will likely surprise the homeowners!

raccoons will fight to protect their kits! Raccoons can also pass on deadly **diseases**, like rabies. Rabies is a disease of the nervous system that, when not treated in time, can kill. Raccoons' solid waste carries a tiny worm that can also cause people to get very sick.

Locking or chaining trash cans can help keep raccoons from getting into your garbage.

URBAN SAFARI

Raccoons often sleep during the day and come out at night to search for food, but that is not always the case. The more raccoons there are living somewhere, the easier it is to spot them. They are not shy!

Raccoon footprints look a bit like little handprints.

Raccoons have long toes, and their footprints are easy to spot. They look a little like human handprints. Raccoons also make a big mess when searching for food and making dens. You will likely find spilled garbage cans, ruined gardens, and broken bird feeders in neighborhoods where raccoons live.

GLOSSARY

ADAPTED (uh-DAPT-ed) Changed to fit new conditions.

COMPOST PILES (KOM-pohst PYLZ) Mixtures of decaying matter, such as leaves, used as fertilizer.

DISEASES (dih-ZEEZ-ez) Illnesses or sicknesses.

GRUBS (GRUBZ) Insects in an early stage of growth.

HIBERNATE (HY-bur-nayt) To spend the winter in a sleeplike state.

LITTERS (LIH-terz) Groups of animals born to the same mother at the same time.

MAMMALS (MA-mulz) Warm-blooded animals that have a backbone and hair, breathe air, and feed milk to their young.

MATING (MAYT-ing) Coming together to make babies.

OMNIVORES (OM-nih-vorz) Animals that eat both plants and animals.

PREY (PRAY) An animal that is hunted by another animal for food.

PROTECTIVE (pruh-TEK-tiv) Having to do with keeping something or someone from being hurt.

INDEX

WEB SITES

For Web resources related to the subject of this book,
go to: www.windmillbooks.com/weblinks
and select this book's title.